gutter rainbows

gutter rainbows

melissa eleftherion

Querencia Press – Chicago IL

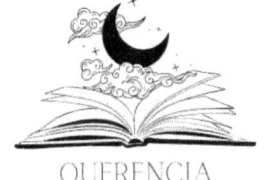

QUERENCIA

QUERENCIA PRESS

© Copyright 2024
Melissa Eleftherion

All Rights Reserved

ISBN 978 1 963943 03 0

.

www.querenciapress.com

First Published in 2024

Querencia Press, LLC
Chicago IL

Printed & Bound in the United States of America

ALSO BY MELISSA ELEFTHERION

field guide to autobiography
abject sutures
sunflower spell
abalone
trauma suture
little ditch
green grass asterisms
the leaves the leaves
Pigtail Duty
prism maps
huminsect

"Melissa Eleftherion has conjured a spectral labyrinth of psyche and precision. The poems in this collection oscillate between the visceral and the ethereal, exploring themes of identity, desire, and existential yearning with linguistic play that is both brutal and beautiful....Here, human experiences crystallize, reflecting natural beauty and human intervention—the cuts that form gems out of us, the fractures defining our most intimate landscapes....This collection is for anyone who has felt their own fractures, who has been both mineral and sculptor in the relentless pursuit of self-definition."

—MK Chavez, winner of the Pen Oakland Josephine Miles award & author of *Dear Animal.*

"I love Melissa Eleftherion's *gutter rainbows*: the surprises, the intelligence, and the human stories attached to all of it. "No one owns a body," she writes, and yet the works recursively connect human to natural realms. This is a book I will return to, just to see how the poet crafts these miracles."

—Denise Low, author & Kansas Poet Laureate Emerita

"I've always delighted in the accumulated moments, rushes, staggers, staccatos and fragments of Melissa Eleftherion's propulsive lyric. There is such a delight of sound and rhythm, and *gutter rainbows* is awash with the best of what her work simultaneously provides: an anxious calm, fine precision and concussive force. Her poems are akin to the ocean: as vast and dangerous as it is deep."

—rob mclennan, author & publisher for above/ground press

Dedicated to my mom & the Brooklyn friends who saw me through: Theresa, Faye Leilanie, Chrissy, Tatesha, Denise, Stefani, & Chris.

To the magic & grit of Coney Island.

Dedicated to teens everywhere.

.

*In every part of every living thing
is stuff that once was rock*

*In blood the minerals
of the rock—*

"*Lake Superior,*" *Lorine Niedecker*

CONTENTS

gasp

Brighton Beach

sea-worn glass smoothed by ocean mouth
we wandered into your opening for
so long we forgot streetlight curfew

the gunmetal tide an invitation
i swam in the hot sludge of summer

swirling styrofoam oily with hair gel
and the grit of defiant refuse

i refused
the heat between my legs a warning

my kindling was my own   heart
little lit matches held

chamber by chamber

green glass flowers

fleshed from the portal's eye
ravenous/in\pieces
the stems littled
silenced sepals /up the steeple
up up they wilt
skinned pinafores
gash of pigtails
murmurs & decay
the /ditch\ calls

blister

pink ditch in wilderness
gash in the ground
damp & rent with salt
no one owns a body

Staten Island, 1982

gutter flower

I was on roller-skates holding on

the curb was high   i climbed
                                                     and climbed

humping a couch arm

little girl legs

make   quiet

where   Madonna   statue

witnessed   harm

tugging the line

taut between bodies

swabbed   sting of rubbing   testing

pre-teen ditch

rough hair unwashed & slept in   a face i mouthed under in
little stab gasps big skins rubbing against   thighs and little girl
leggings a misfit interrogation they were at the window   panic
          in a crescendo of flapping i crossed the street mouths hung
open lemon yellow laughter   the i of taking it like a meat girl

nipples   flapping

asphalt   skins

a glow of calling—   streetlights

a ditch in pink wilderness

                                   meat girl is grief

cut off   peeled bark
                                    dull hums

The ditch is a teenage girl
the girl is a ditch
all the little inserts
the pink gooey centers
what hardens inside

A girl is a gash is a rut
is sore knees
a bedtime story a lullaby of woundings
how the little matches strike
a calling a namesake
what the blood culls

GUTTER FLOWER

eight-year-old girl   on the sidewalk playing jacks
          there a box of leftover porn   there, there
daddy

eleven-year-old girl   at the diner in a halter dress
b e c k o n in g man's licking lips

fourteen-year-old girl, walking   the avenue of eyeballs an
OTB sideshow   the curdling gawk & greased
taunts
          it counted cement boxes

sixteen-year-old girl   staged in a wet tee shirt
          its nipples hung, grit &
sobbing   rubbing the after   bourbon &
bathroom graffiti

seventeen-year-old girl   the aborted summer sun   the
slapping   a witness   a hole in the door

          it left a body   it left a killing jar

it left its body   there   in the dirt lot   there, there

crows

hoarse & cawing
wild voice
in the elder   arms around you

black & black as aglow makes
thunder cracks branches

how startling   the revolt

has not   claimed us

sooner

black & black

                  as voice does

the reckoning cry above

its stealth   and wingspan

a breath we take in

the heart   a molt
of feathers   and expansion   we move   in trees

                              swoop

    our mouths are

    to the ground
                    feeding

the interiority of female misogyny

it was the toughness
i faked

whcn wc sct firc to thc woods
when we threw beer bottles in the stream
and when
we tagged the subway car at 65th Street

it was the metal breathing
when we made out with boys in your basement
when we followed that girl every day after school, taunting
when we danced in the pit & went home bruised

i lied

it all hurt
and i had to go

the toughness   /   & i dismissed

          was a catalyst

Cave
where the ocean broke
in tiny waves
it came crashing

Avuncular

Uncle Olly doesn't know any better

It's up to me to set the tone

It's up to me to say no

The pond in the condo development

the stained gold cushions in YiaYia's condo

Stale Winstons in the middle of the night

Uncle Olly's room

Porn on the walls

Uncle Olly supine on the couch

Relaxed dopey smile as he stares at the ceiling

moving his head back and forth

Uncle Olly pointing to me then

to the porn poster then to himself   eye gleam   giggles

I am 12 I am 15 I am 9

Uncle Olly didn't know any better

It was up to me to set the tone

Uncle Olly gesturing Uncle Olly gesturing to me and then to

himself Uncle Olly

gesturing to me and then to himself and then eye gleam reaches

It was daytime and the shame of taking off my shirt in the hot sun

The blonde girl

The blonde girl on the poster

The blonde girl on the poster on the wall looking down at me

It was summertime

ruby-throated hummingbird

They say you're common
but not to a Brooklyn girl like me
The only ruby flutterings of my youth
traffic lights under the El
as we raced to the dun waters
of the Bay (behind bars)

My own red mouth agape
in the backseat listening
to my parents fight
Little Red Corvette on the radio
My only adult male
a hostile boil
that wiped out the bank accounts
My hum a landscape
for displacement
or
where do you go when tectonics shift
when the rocking boat lifts
& nothing is where
you left it
not even the skin
that carried you
on the ferris wheel that night
the whir & candy
the faces all lit up in neon

You looked down
at your brother
put your feelings
between the boardwalk slats
The yelling lost in the din
The quarters in your palm
As you looked out
at the Atlantic
& saw
your first loon.

asnakemetrical

Allure of echinoderm symmetry
We marveled gasping in sea[wage] wa[te]r

Mom applied vigor
At the attachment a variation

We were trees, we were leaves, we were litter
This habit of margins
No scientific names found

Long, divided—but extending
We chased balloons in the rain
Developed unique body plans

If I tattoo you with flowers, it will be a kind of protection
If I eat Lays with Grandma, it will be connection
We avoided the porn, adjusted the Craftmatic

Distinguished from other brittle stars
Distinguished from the bottom-dweller

The rapture of pentaradial force
The wrath of a sessile ancestor

Oh, calcareous fatty deposits
Oh, carton of YiaYia's Winstons
Yellow calla lilies callow in the breeze

We wanted a gut of snakes
We wanted a mouth teeming with stars

the leaves the leaves

a green that grows
in the cracks
four inches tall and full
of wet
don't ask me
to be a girl
long, front legs &
carapace of sutures
one stitch for each
net-veined leaf
one attempt
at a community of animals
the sticking of webs
jelly louse interstice
one revolution past
known fidelities
i was a girl then
in the stitches
my own thinking, a glow ghost
my familiar, a heart
cast by injuries
i sealed them in chambers
little green
in the cracks
little earths
of roaring lotus
a gentle wind stoking

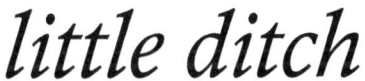

little ditch

New Utrecht

                                                    the fire was
                        and so i slept with it

tying my white tee   up in the summer heat

i bounced to the sidewalk   to my boyfriend's fist

"you're   not   a   guy.   it's different

        girls   have   to   wear   shirts"

                                        the vertigo.

                                            why this kind
of fire

        i was my self until i was a self being myself

                                            <avoid self
fill the boyfriend hole>
                                            the i i tucked
and tucked

            "do i really have to use a condom"

he stole in   and astride   my sleeping   cadavered

    torso   in   slumber   i   called

    to   i

    murmurs   warm   murmurs   force

    i came up to the knife   flipped his angry

purpled

    body beneath mine   and taunted
his

freckles with the blade

i snuck out

4 am headache in a
diner booth—our legs
thin teenage sticks
of longing
beneath the table
we smoked and drank burnt coffee in
chipped, white ceramic mugs
our ashes tipping over the
tinfoil ashtray
crying and laughing into
our disco fries

Self-Esteem

We held hands beneath the dirt
We wanted to be trees
Disintegration was all we could ask for
We embraced in the ditch
Our eyelashes caked in dirt
We were a burial
We were roots
We created our own boundary
Every moment of it entangled
The blood we carried

Leaves a cadence
Veins your laughter catching the light
When sorrow wept who wiped its stars
Sidereal sidewalk imaginary
We engrave ourselves in cement when we feel lost
We cackle and stutter the cracks in the asphalt landscape
My home my playground my rubble
Who will tell the leaves they make lovely gravel

i am a doll dug out of a landfill

Body of the cave mouth

Dissolution of salt

Intuitive ash collects

i vibrate to the speleothem the duodenum

My heart holds the dirt

like some sweet music

i remember once a breathing green

i remember once breathing

i am a dull dig out of a landscape

The hemisphere a polydactyl crustacean of a fault

Veil of topography how the dirt is lucid mass
shell of sea star fall

in a ditch this sun's
channel lines and gaps

Here i am that dirt

i am limestone I am gravel

Lush grave of the verdant flesh

a lyric from the detritus

One lyric

up up little ascending

i say this to my cohort i say to the wind

my desert of doll people i say to the abandoned tire i say

to metal

up up you can reach it

individuation

it was the wildness
everything was singing and
you tried to protect me
i resisted   it was pitch
and forest it was the trenches

i washed my mud and
donned its mother i slept
among the trees my golden guilt

it was the wild nests of
brooklyn summer it was the
cyclone everything was grit
and sunshine a glitter
of dun sand. what is protection
he asked under the boardwalk
who rides the wonder wheel

i resisted   it was milk
or the ditch
so i started digging.

Great Kills

there was a sliding glass door leading to the backyard we didn't own but was egress to a fourteen yr old girl seeking escape from premature adulthood a bat's constant flapping

i snuck out in love with the cloak of stars roller-skating on the slick streets of a rundown suburban gaslight tunnel i took a pre-paid cab to your father's mansion in the middle of the night out the glass door out of the landfill of Great Kills

i sought the damage in you i fed it to my heart i applied it like a sealant i searched for your sadness to warm my sadness i craved your striptease worship the caresses of two boys at once i turned milk with longing and satisfaction i wanted to believe i deserved love i resisted intuition like a cloying parent

love was dirt in the mouth
my face in the cake
the slapping   the soothing

love was lies and lies
love was two against one
the red blinking eye of his video-camera

there was a sliding glass door leading to the rented backyard where i lay out all night talking about universal mysteries with my neighbor supine & starry-eyed on top of a picnic table awaiting sunrise

the glass door i slipped through & into the night too anxious to sleep the irregularities of my skins and their seams not fitting quite right i look up and the moon seams back at me a reassuring presence we glide together i began to learn how to be alone how to stay and fight how to walk through glass & pretend to be unscathed

there was a sliding glass door that connected my bedroom to a way out and i was free all those times even when it was obvious i was breakage

ditchwitch

origin of the cave

slowly seeping water

woman excavates

her mouth

from the ditch

dirt lot

feral girl who took to the woods yes we hopped off that bus as it left
the rotting pit of Staten Island, that neon pit utopia of boredom

nostalgia   i ate it slaked in mud the rotting garbage patch of
my suburban commerce i slaked the mud over my lips a wanting to
enter you as the rain fell on your raincoat how you laid it down over
the compost ditch we fucked on the slaking we caked it clawing mud
pit i left the bus willingly   as if to feel some kind of love

years and years the news called and green lines gold the perimeter a
rabbit of time sounded   they had found your body in those
woods   what was left of your youth then as four days passed and
years and miles of myopia burned the residue i fell away

despite the distance my body lies in those woods our haven our place
   it was mine too you cannot claim it   you lied   that space
was wanting and within the wanting was my body   left there in
the dictum of my making a blood cull from the talons of star fuselage
wrecked atoms of my fueled mist and now i am smoke

you culled me from mud and wilderness i eat it my heart i eat it
microbiota i salvage it from the pit of longing that was my tccnagc
wilderness a clawing up an errant mouth of wounds a moth how
tender the flaking of its gossamer and fuck you wings i slicked you
like the vulnerable pink you were soft tissue and rupture is glisten
          as i move   the shovel   with my   foot and aim
   the dirt   for your mouth

bury bury dirt lot utopia bury bury the margins i split open on that
line a slit of shimmering lies

little ditch

little ditch was a century
                [shh don't startle the ash]
little ditch is a call to armor
                [shh don't stir the bottom]

this is a wake for the ashes   this is an attempt to
convene with the memory of the
interruption   please startle all the ashes   ancestors of
stitches

i took up my silence in your mouth
all those nights i lied so i could forget
i fled i kept coming back i pumped my legs high on the swing and
hoped
all those days we were one home one body
i climbed over dog shit and pizza boxes to hold your hand

there was the light that day off the fire escape and you were
crying
when i consoled you the truth in the gleam off the window your
open crooked mouth i fell in

i slept in your bed all those years there was no other bed
but betrayal and for that piece i fought others like me
teased hair and fist-fights   rumors and rank-outs stealing
bruises and
romanticizing little boy pains i lost hid concealed ate my own
i pretended i was one of the cool girls i'm not a cool girl anymore
i'm a cunt

little ditch was a century   a lineage of oppressed
women of institutionalized women of internalized hatred
of sadness and separation of spit and rage and claws
of woman against woman of a perpetual lie

little ditch is centuries of digging

little dig dig product
little dig dig consume
little dig dig insidious grey pallor fog in the bloodstream a defect
in the cell division a slash across the ribs

little ditch is a burned-out Barbie Dream House sour milk
between legs a motor that guns every time she tries to speak
casually interrupted in conversation
casually sexually assaulted in conversation casually dismissed
gaslit

little ditch tried to be a good girl bounced on men's knees when
told/don't bite back bit instead the insides of cheeks to taste her
own blood/remembering her worth—pennies

                    the dirt in her mouth
                    one small sacrifice
                    —her wobbly arms doin' the wop
                    her belly fat exhaled in a curdle atop

little tight dresses little bow ties little ditch started young
she took it all in opened her mouth wide lips cracked
she became walls

little ditch body

traded belly & the trees

armor landscape

the become

little cleavage light

gravity of small forms

burial ground rotting pink

girl   glass   mouth

We hid in the culverts

tunneled our way out

all was golden

in the woods

until we

noticed

how close

we were

to the mall

when we emerged

all was sewage plant landscape

cemetery landscape

the ditch of capitalism

i spent the rest

of my time

seeking a way back underground

Self-Portrait as Used Condom Riding the Wonder Wheel

little
　i'm story
of light and cleavage

in the gutter
a symmetry of fractures

radial Brooklyn
its minerals and bubblegum tar

its sidewalk a rub of bellies and salt
its sidewalk a trust of grit and glamor
a friend

a beast, capitalism
colorless lie of dead habit

a radial I am from

proteins of light   disrapture

rot and implacable rust

interregnum salts

claw and ghost

　a beam of rage

i am the small parts

thumb sparrow   a sprout in the hand

no goldenrod no daisy

i am the little wheel

splinter

little matchstick

follicle   i got past the cleaving

past the interregnum

the small parts at dawn

glisten in the crackle

half meat   half thunder

i am leaf vein

leaf matter

leaf at rest

gill

the separation of wounds matter

the gentle splits

little stem

resist parental tyranny
their many skins slippery
their many branches
rotting, swelled
little stem, little oblongata

little combat flower
be strong in the overture
in the wave crash
too many shouting men
be strong be bold

yes yes
little feral
moving
into
yes light
the wolf
the war

gutter maps

ocean ellipsis mouth
we catch ourselves
a grumble in the time gap
maw's energetic swallow
her beast, her quickening

where were all the murderous
bowlegged dangers i avoided
roller-skating down Mermaid Avenue
back when tides washed the back legs of youth's agency

there in the subatomic catacomb
an organism of prisms
sold in the back junk shops

i washed my poverty in anonymous
erotic paperbacks i washed
my ideas about poverty through
the camera's ground glass

the smiling was a circle
i swung to—the sun
beat the boardwalk and its

nostalgic catastrophe of magics
a map of gaslight gutter
rainbows i followed to the sea

cleavage

cleavage (n.) the tendency of a mineral to break in smooth, flat planes; a fundamental property of a mineral [due to its relation] to the atomic arrangement of the crystal

How we break is a primary identifying characteristic
What are the ways in which you are broken?

This is the species of sediment
These are the leaks of fossils

Milky and weathered
These brittle spheres of light

Through the glass cleavage
I dissolve in acid

This is the story of my formation
Monoclinic symmetry

Chrysoberyl

becoming violet-red
in artificial light
brittle boundaries
in the schismatics
found jagged
in the cleavage remains of luster
but the hardness,
a gravity
when such a stone
is cut
to form
a gem

hematite

The red streak is the most important test
to be variously distinguished
& considered common
a natural occurrence
How the scarlet marks

The measure
in mammillary growths
No cleavage but
in iron-bearing

Scales in magnetic weather
a blurring of oxides
Igneous gravity a man-made hide
Run now with your red earth

the puberty of rocks

We were the soft faces
Dull & hardened a fissure
A conchoidal gravity

The skins oh the roses and browns and veins
We were in the scaly light so long we burned the specimens

A grassy mouthing
A hush grace
We were in the charade
We waved to the fluorescing

How the perfect cleavage distinguishes
Even in minerals
Rocks and their greasy fractures

How all this learning about breaking
is really a kind of longing
The smell his leaving left on the fire escape
We were little sticks

marcasite

The fractures are uneven

Where you hid the groceries
Where you hid the wailing

Shifting plates

Become
Where a shell escapes

Become familial
<its own terrors>

Little islands
<even the paper tectonics>

In the brass morning light
Sex was on the walls

In the quiet
In the radiation

Little rusted springs

In the vestibular
A weary grown together

Matches & dust

Little springs intergrown
From tabular parallels

Your family becomes my family
A child becomes a homing device

Some solution takes place here
Diluted gases in the cooling

Chaoite

Dark grey mass

Shock-metamorphosed

From meteorite

You abrade

Easily

Scale off memory of impact—

                    Your shell

                    Not so hard it crumbles

                    Not so vulnerable it shatters

Resilience   a specimen of the long game

Polymorphous—a learned behavior for trauma

Crystals have such nice faces

In a family of diamonds

Sub-metallic lustre

Your allotropic

Double consciousness

White carbon

Thin bones

Gypsum

Hardness, vigilance

Let the throat tell you

In cavities   in caves   in a *massive bed* of rocks

i live in limestone   a crystallized habit

        bend but lack   *bend but lack*

        scratched with fingernails i am tested

        mined for commercial use

these humans soluble in hot acid

        a white precipitate

pearly   silky   fractures

after firing

a long-wave ultraviolet light

calcite

in the cavities i'm colorless
hot like a rotting tooth
i become new forms
concretion among the fading druse
vitreous as cut glass
i effervesce
but how i fracture
is witness
to all that petrifying

Childrenite

pink ditches   a line of semen
we're taught to hold space for the lion
sit quiet at his table
in his car
his house
his wife
palm the childrenite
its uneven fractures a balm
to dissociated fragments
acicular tombs i carry
recur and hostage connections
a vitreous compound
a prismatic habit
the salts i keep sprinkling over a burial

ammonite sonnet

the ammonite an index of sutures
i got tired of cataloging them
hermetically sealing little traumas
afraid they'd get to know one another go boom
little mother catastrophes instead
i smashed little rocks to bits in a ditch
each shard a memory released pressure
from stomach the common burial ground
the cavity of accumulation
each little box coated in dust and feelings
each glass stone chamber not really secret
i get ready to shatter the discretions
i open my palms no explosions no pain
coalesce little traumas wrap your wounds
around each other a chrysalis blood
a becoming of feathers of air a fire

Asphalt

Our Earth's crust   our very foundation

      tells a story

hegemony

            dominion

      injustice and the conquered

All bond to the silicate daddy

as a kid i lay on the burnt Brooklyn sidewalk

looking for beauty in the asphalt

      the little buds that grow from the cracks

      the many shoots of marble and gutter

      all minerals rising to the surface

      fighting to be seen beneath

      the bubblegum tar

      each sidewalk square erupting

      with an ecosystem

how breathing happens watching

    crystals form

how the posturing continues

deep within the molt and rock and plunder

    the dominion of gutter politics how we still

    root for the wounded for a wash of new memory

    so the crystals will rise   pure as salt

chalcedony

the gentle subtlety of true light breaks
arrests then *aggregates radiating*
how the glow extends to us despite our faults

milk blue gravity of
crystal life system   your gap symmetry a balance of victories
moss agate   the nacreous imagine   stalactite   a petrified
wood for lovers

how you hover as transformation
                    in the interstices
          warrior, queen

          your magnanimity
a wonder seeking air

rose quartz

Aureole threshold

is totem

Three smooth vitreous points

Fibrous & *generally stable in ultraviolet light*

One is found or one finds oneself

Irradiation forms dusky hues

Rock crystal asterism

My terminal bud

In each hardness a prism or vein

A loathsome pustule

A bubblegum center

A dichroic future of bilateral symmetries

Our stars pulsing under the stone

Apatite

i am misleading

indistinct, variable

brown to pink to clear

lustrous, vitreous to the dullest

little brittle fracture

mostly transparent

              then opaque

i'm colorless in that

i'm a spectrum

"i contain multitudes"

by turns white, i'm gray

i'm a yellowish green

comprised by all

these valuable radiances

I'm my own supergroup

So various I shine—*a series of related minerals*

The Greeks call me deceptive

But I decode their pyramidal system

i diaphanate like RoyGBiv

Moody af

I'm all hardness—sometimes they say dull

My colloform habit

No   *visible*   *crystalline*
affinities

Comprised of calcium phosphorous hydrogen chlorine oxygen fluorine

I'm "what a girl wants, what a girl needs"

Sharp-tongued and limber enough to keep 'em forever on their toes

A conchoidal fracture developed in the breath of witness

Aurostibite

i'm not radioactive   there's a horizon over my grimace
          lead grey no gammas protuberant teeth
the sonogram catches my gravity

diploidal i'm a star symbol a fracture among the shimmer
my crystal system two TIE fighters on the wind
a metallic streak

Au get off my diaphaneity
What I lack in sulfur I make up in cell dimension
666 – mark of the beast
Good luck getting at my cleavage

kletic

wild mouths wild mouths

when the agor settles

when gold dust lament

covers it all

i am a beetle captured

in glass

my green thorax aglow

among the amber

my pincers akimbo

like come at me bro

i still believe in a female god

Eileithyia

Eileithyia   the bringer   goddess of birth and labor
blonde ringleted child who pulled my hair
my friend my double   we were wicked sprites

our eyes arrest in photographs   our parents doting   our
friends
envious we were inseparable   we were a sacred cave

It was night   a knock at the door
I hid my treasures   crouched behind sofa cushions

Eileithyia's mother crying   kneeling on our doorstep
My father firmly shaking his head   then handing her a
plastic bag of powder

We had come from caves   I wasn't allowed in
your home
Your bell was broken so I'd pelt   your window with
gravel bits
Dream of climbing up your fire Escape desire so palpable

      Myth says you are the Mother of Eros
      You were the mother of mine

Before I understood the war of misogyny
      I battled my   own blood for understanding

I fought and bled for answers I slept with all my ancestors
and killed the dreams between my legs how the antlers
char when war consumes

I took war into my mouth and spat wrath in a
cataclysm of ash my   organisms subsumed in it

Mother of Eros Mother of Ash
We bled from sea to sea

Eileithyia warrior of the coy and fecund daughter of screams
I sublimated   my desire   in shopping malls
& in the schoolyard
In wood-paneled basements   in suburban rec rooms
        in the sprawl of the casual   i adopted to pretend
myself expansive
When making out with the drummer the bassist the drummer
again the singer the singer the singers

I learned to loathe my kind so early i breathed it in like a costume
i could not take off
The holiday tantrums and trauma headaches of eros in my young
mouth
A cunt I could not fathom for its endless spun of mortal vigor
The death cycle of skin under the fluorescents skins in the dark
deathbed room skins sagged ungraceful and exhausted the black
circle where I do not forgive you

Mother in Caves   Mother Limestone
        Mother of Carbon   Mother of Magma

dichroic

her story is my story is your story the axes we intersect, collide,
ruminate, devise
the branches we extend to heartache to the larynx to the mouth
humans in our filth and consequence partially digested morals
and transformative butt yoga
we allied in flesh and rattles a kindred of sextants making sense of
pecuniary disease a systemic longing for connections when
criminal justice is criminal warfare and we are all under this rock
heaving against it with our might intact and our eyes xanthic with
exhaustion. we are in this radial of desire we dichroic points &
light when we turn we turn together and that's where we're going

Acknowledgments & Notes

I wish to extend my heartfelt gratitude to the editors of the following publications in which poems in Gutter Rainbows previously appeared:

Poems from little ditch were released as the chapbook *little ditch* (above/ground press, 2018).

"ammonite sonnet" first appeared in *Arsenic Lobster* & was featured in *Voicemail Poems.*

"Aurostibite" first appeared in *Bone Bouquet.*

"kletic" first appeared in *Burning House Press' No Machine without a Ghost.*

"chalcedony" first appeared in *Chaudiere Books.*

"New Utrecht" first appeared in *Delirious Hem.*

"Gypsum" first appeared in *Dream Pop.*

"Chrysoberyl" first appeared in *Dusie.*

"Individuation" first appeared as "ditch poem #20" in *Ethel.*

"Eileithyia" first appeared in *Feral: A Journal of Poetry & Art.*

"hematite" first appeared in *Flag & Void.*

"Childrenite" first appeared in *Gigantic Sequins.*

"Brighton Beach" first appeared in *Headline Poetry & Press.*

"the puberty of rocks" first appeared in *inter/rupture*.

"ruby-throated hummingbird" first appeared in *Italian-Americana Review*.

"pre-teen ditch", "crows" & "dirt lot" first appeared in *LUNA LUNA*. "dirt lot" also appeared in the anthology *Poet-Librarians in the Library of Babel* (2017).

"gutter maps" first appeared in *Lunch Ticket*.

"Self-Portrait as Used Condom Riding the Wonder Wheel" first appeared in *The Maynard*.

"Asphalt" first appeared in *Mi-Go Zine*.

"GUTTER FLOWER" first appeared in *NICE CAGE*.

"rose quartz" first appeared in *Periodicities: A Journal of Poetry & Poetics*

"*the leaves the leaves*" first appeared as a micro-chapbook from *Poems-For-All* (2017).

"I snuck out" first appeared in *Postcard Poems and Prose*.

"asnakemetrical" first appeared in *Queen Mobs*.

"the interiority of female misogyny" first appeared in *Rogue Agent*.

The following poems from *little ditch* were featured on *Sundress Publications'* The Wardrobe (2020): "Brighton Beach"; "blister" as "ditch poem # 13" ; "individuation" as "ditch poem #20" ; "little ditch" ; "ammonite sonnet"

"Dichroic" first appeared as "her story is my story is your story" in *SWWIM.*

"Chaoite" first appeared in *TAB Journal.*

"Apatite" first appeared in *The Tiny.*

"i am a doll dug out of a landfill" was featured at *Vallejo Poetry Society*.

The poems "marcasite" & "blister" as "ditch poem #13" first appeared in *Yes, Poetry.*

Thanks so much to the early readers of this work who helped shape it into being: Claire Blotter, Sharon Coleman, & Sherre Vernon. So much gratitude to Denise Low, Rob McLennan, and MK Chavez for their early support & heartfelt blurbs for Gutter Rainbows. Many thanks to Emily Perkovich & Querencia Press for believing in this book.

www.ingramcontent.com/pod-product-compliance
Lightning Source LLC
Chambersburg PA
CBHW071215120626
46546CB00006B/2577